Long Nights Journey
Into Dawn

Ease Your Pain

To Wonderful Peggy

Love and Light,
Sita

Long Nights Journey Into Dawn

Ease Your Pain

Sita Earlyne Chaney, Ph.D.
Illustrations by Peggy Jackson

Astara's Library of Mystical Classics

Published by

Astara

10700 Jersey Blvd., Ste. 450
P.O. Box 2100
Rancho Cucamonga, CA 91729-2100

Astara, Inc.
10700 Jersey Blvd., Ste. 450
P.O. Box 2100
Rancho Cucamonga, CA 91729-2100
www.astara.org

CREDITS:

Editor: Sita Chaney

Cover Design: Elizabeth Hickerson

ISBN 978-0-918936-60-8
Library of Congress Control Number: 2006932212

Printed in the United States of America

About the Author

Dr. Sita Earlyne Chaney is a teacher, writer, counselor and lecturer combining metaphysics, mysticism and modern psychology for practical, everyday use. In addition to her post as Executive Administrator for Astara, she serves as President of Astara's Board of Director-Trustees. She holds academic degrees from both Occidental College and Purdue University and an ordination from Astara.  Her first book, *Memories: My Parents the Mystics* was published in 2003.

Dedication

This book is dedicated to Nina Aronoff, Ph.D., without whose heartfelt help and support I may not have made the long night's journey into dawn. I would also like to thank "Team Sita," the people who are mentioned in Chapter One.

I Would Like To Thank ...

I would like to thank the following people whose behind-the-scenes efforts helped make this book a reality so that I could share with you the wonderful, divine messages which I received as I was recovering from the treatment of my brain tumor. My deep desire is to be nothing but a messenger, sharing this divine guidance with you. It is my hope that this will help you in every way possible.

Peggy Jackson, whose wonderful illustrations highlight every message
Elizabeth Hickerson
Gina Munson
Pam Rau
Dean Zakich
Steve Doolittle

Foreword

A question frequently asked is: "Why do bad things happen to good people?" This question was asked on many occasions by many different people while Dr. Sita Chaney fought the cancer that had invaded her body. But just as the disease fought to gain ground in her body, fear tried to gain ground in her spirit. Her spirit fought the doubts and depression that come while trying to live through a life-threatening situation. Her spirit entered into a state of darkness — the night.

The 13th century poet, Hafiz, wrote, "I wish I could show you, when you are lonely or in darkness, the astonishing Light of your own Being." Just as the medicines fought to eradicate the cancer, the Light of Sita's own Being, and the Light of those sent to assister her, shone brightly to fight against the doubts and fear that threatened to diminish her spirit. The Physical and Spiritual realms balanced and entered into a new state of Being — the dawn.

These are her experiences during her time of darkness and the messages she received from her angels, guides and own Being. By reading them you will walk through the darkness with her, be inspired by her strength, and see the astonishing Light of YOUR own Being. In reading Sita's messages not only will you learn that you are braver than you believe, stronger than you seem, and smarter than you think; but most importantly, you will learn that you are truly loved and never alone. As Sita, would say, "Read on, Dear Reader, read on."

Dr. Jill Porter
June, 2006

Chapter One
Long Nights Journey Into Dawn

Dear reader, you may be familiar with the first line of a classic novel written by Charles Dickens. The novel is *A Tale of Two Cities*. The novel begins with the first line saying, "It was the best of times, it was the worst of times." Even though I was an English major in college, I never really knew what that line meant until I went through a terrible physical trauma and came out of it. It was the worst of times for me, which has now led to the best of times. Thank you for the clarification, Mr. Dickens!

Before I was diagnosed with a brain tumor, I was relatively healthy. I went to my general practitioner annually for physicals. But suddenly, when I was forty-two years old, I woke up one morning and thought, "Why are there two ceilings up there?" What I had was double vision, and gradually it got worse over time. My left eye simply would not turn to the left, as is normal. I had to start wearing a black eye patch, which made me look like a pirate. I went to my eye doctor, who examined my eyes. I had 20/20 vision. In fact, I still do. He told me not to worry. He said seven out of ten people who get this condition, get it because of a stressful situation. He did send me to get an MRI, without contrast, which found nothing.

Since I wasn't under any particular stress at the time, I simply thought nothing of it. My eye very oddly kept turning more and more toward the center of my face and simply refused to budge.

Thankfully, I had no pain or severe headaches due to any of this. But a year after this had first started, I went back to my general practitioner for my annual checkup. She said, "Look, Sita, this has gone on way too long. I think you should go see a neurologist." I did. The neurologist, gave me another MRI, this time with contrast. From the results of this test my brain tumor was diagnosed. At that point the doctors told me I had to move very quickly. The MRI indicated that it was located in a place in my brain where I could not have surgery. I very quickly had to start chemotherapy and radiation treatments. Suddenly I had to go from one visit to my general practitioner a year to seven weeks, five days a week of radiation treatments and chemotherapy. It certainly was the worst of times for me.

But, dear reader, enough about me. Suffice it to say, that I eventually came out of this using traditional medical treatments, as well as various forms of alternative treatments and healing, which all united to help me get well. During my treatment and healing I was surrounded by wonderful people. They loved, took care of, encouraged, and supported me in every way. They jokingly called themselves Team Sita. And I regularly give thanks for each of them in my life. I give thanks also for all the love and prayers from other dear friends as well. Team Sita included my wonderful Daddy, Robert Chaney, Nina Aronoff, Ph.D., Susan Regas, Ph.D. and Steve Doolitttle. Without them, and other dear friends in my life I never would have made it. But this book, dear reader, is not really about me.

The wonderful Jungian psychologist, writer, speaker, Jean Shinoda-Bolen, M.D., has informed us that often people who go through any kind of head trauma, whether it be a brain tumor, a car accident, or some other type of incident, often become more psychically and intuitively alert. The brain is often rattled enough that we start to hear spiritual voices at times. Voices from On High, I would call them. Now please know I'm not talking about psychotic voices. I do have a Ph.D. in marriage and family therapy. Frankly it only takes common sense to tell the difference between some psychotic message (for example, "God told me I should go kill my neighbor because he doesn't mow his lawn properly.") and a truly spiritual psychic message, which is sent to us from On High. I believe all of us are psychic but sometimes we need a little push to help us open the door and receive the messages from above.

This book is about the messages that I received as my healing process really began in earnest. These messages were sent to me by my Master Teachers, guardian angels, and by my dear, sweet Mom, Earlyne Chaney, to help push me towards total strength and healing. But I don't believe that these messages are just for me. I'm sure they are meant to help those of you who have been through any of life's ups and downs. Not simply physical trauma, but emotional trauma, difficulties in a relationship, or the trauma of trying to stay on your spiritual path in spite of what life may throw in front of you. So, come along with me, dear reader, as I share these messages with you, and the meaning I received from them, which have helped me immensely, and which I am very hopeful could be of great help to you, also.

I began receiving these messages after going through treatment and dealing with all the side effects which chemo, radiation and the brain tumor had given me. My hair had grown back, after having completely fallen out from chemotherapy. I had started to be able to eat again, after going through about a year and a half simply not being able to eat at all. I was only able to drink Ensure Plus to try to maintain a bit of my weight. So, I had my hair back, and a bit of my appetite had returned, when I received my first message.

The voice that I heard came to me right inside my head. It was not like sitting, talking to someone and hearing what that person has to say. It seemed as though there was someone inside my own head talking, or as in my case, usually singing. Those wonderful, divine spirits from On High who were sending me messages certainly knew how best to reach me so that I would pay attention and hear them. Those of you who are reading this book who are interested in poetry for example, may get a message using a line from a favorite poem. Or, if you are an avid TV watcher, a line from a favorite TV show may simply, suddenly be heard in your head. Well, dear reader, I happen to love music. I grew up with a favorite hobby of my sweet Mama, who also loved music. She recorded song after song on reel to reel tapes, and played them throughout the house regularly. Because of this, I know the lyrics to lots of different songs, and so the spiritual beings used song lyrics to send me their messages. They made sure I knew the difference between my own thoughts and a message which is sent to me from On High. These messages most often take the form of a song lyric, coming from a song which I have not thought of nor heard in years. This is simply their way to make the point that I should pay attention to what they're trying to tell me.

So the first message came to me when, finally my hair had grown back, and I had started to eat once again. Thus, I looked a bit better than I had been looking, and I had begun gaining a little weight.

The first message came to me one morning actually in November, 2003, when I was brushing my teeth. I looked in the mirror and thought, "Oh my God – I'm looking more and more similar to what I used to look like." After I looked at myself in the mirror and thought that, I just continued to brush my teeth. Morning oblutions, as they are called.

All of a sudden, from out of the blue, the song *Hello Dolly* began playing in my head —

"Hello Dolly
Well, hello Dolly,
It's so nice to have you back where you belong
You're looking swell Dolly,
We can tell, Dolly,
You're still glowin', you're still crowin',
    you're still goin' strong
We feel the room swayin'
For the band's playin'
One of your old favorite songs from way back
    when
So, Golly gee fellows, find me a vacant knee
    fellows,
    Dolly will never go away again"

When I thought about the lyrics to this wonderful song, they did take on added significance to me. I felt as though my conscious self was coming back into my body. My body was becoming a bit more normal. In terms of the lyrics, too, I oftentimes did feel the room swaying because radiation damage had knocked off my equilibrium completely. I am working hard to rebuild strength and balance on the right side of my entire body which has become rather weak. Also, I do focus a lot of attention on bending my right knee at the appropriate time to improve my ability to walk.

So, dear reader, I did just want to confirm that this wonderful song is one I had not thought of nor heard in years. And the wonderful, Divine Spirits upstairs were confirming that I was slowly coming back into my body, where I belonged. They were confirming that I had begun to look better, and I felt that they were telling me definitely that the brain tumor was not going to begin growing again. Thus I would not be going away again into my illness. So please know that any trauma that you have been through, be it physical, emotional/relationship trauma, or spiritual, you, too, can go through it and get back to where you belong. You may well need a team of loving people around you, and the power of the prayers of those who love you, no matter how far away geographically they may be. Plus the wonderful, Divine Spirits On High are doing their best to help you go through this difficult time, as well. Just know, dear reader, whatever it is, you can make it, and they'll be upstairs smiling and singing, "Hello, it's so nice to have you back where you belong."

Chapter Two
Hey, Big Spender

Well, the second message I received occurred a week or two after the first. This message, once again, came to me in the morning just after I was waking up. Now believe me, these messages are not part of a dream when I lay fast asleep. They usually came when I was alert enough to grasp them, but had not yet started the minute by minute, active routine of the day. Thus, my focus was a bit inward and I was feeling rather serene before my day started. Apparently any time we are not active with our day-to-day routine, and our focus is turned a bit inward, rather than totally outward, it is often the best moment for our guardian angels or our Master Teachers to reach us. Such was often the case with me. They knew just when to knock on the door of my consciousness so that I could actually receive the message they were sending. I am sure that over time I have missed quite a few of the messages they have sent, but the ones I became aware of I would like to share with you. It is my hope, as I have said before, that they will assist you with any of the ups and downs of life, no matter what those may be for you.

This second message I received were some of the lyrics of a song from Mama's generation. The song was called *Big Spender*. They'd often find a way to change a word or two for me, to really emphasize the true message they were sending. The message I received was as follows:

"The minute you walked in the joint
I could see you were a gal of distinction,
A real big spender.
Hey, big spender,
Spend a little time with me"

Now, of course, what they said to me in the second line was "you were a gal of distinction." The correct lyrics are, "I could tell you were a man of distinction." Since, of course, I'm not a man, they were using every means possible to let me know that this was a message for me and not simply a song I was remembering.

These lyrics have many meanings. Some of the words from the first line are "the minute you walked..." As I wrote in the previous chapter, the radiation I had to endure, and the nerve damage from my brain tumor had thrown my equilibrium off totally. I often felt almost like I was surfing. So when they send me a message regarding walking, it is extremely meaningful to me. I took it to be a message conveying to me that I will be able to actually walk normally again, but I'd need to really work at it.

When I got down to the part of the lyrics calling me "a real big spender, hey big spender," that does not mean that one of my habits before this health trauma was spending a lot of money. What I did spend was my time and effort to be helpful to other people. For example, I spent at least fifteen years of my life as a marriage and family therapist helping client after client repair their relationship as best as possible. Or if they desired it, if it was best for them to break up, I attempted to help them part amicably, with as much friendship as possible. I would also spend some time on an Astara tour to spiritual sites around the world, or during Astara's Spiritual Ceremonies to simply be a channel asking the pure, white divine spiritual light to come down from the heavens and go through me into any person that was in front of me. Thus I made every effort to be a big spender of spiritual energy, giving it through one ritual or another to others.

The last line of the message I received was, "spend a little time with me." In thinking about this line, I interpreted it to mean that I had spent so much time, effort and energy trying to help other people in different ways that I was neglecting myself in some way. The message was that I should save some of that Divine Power and Energy for me. Yes, I did try to spend some time in meditation regularly. But at this traumatic time in my life, I clearly needed to open and receive the Divine, Sacred energy much more than I was. To me, the line in the song which is, "spend a little time with me" was trying to tell me, "Spend time with us, Sita, we're trying to help you up here, but you've got to do your part of not only opening up and receiving, but channeling that divine, sacred energy into you so that you can once again walk normally."

So, dear reader, my hunch is, whether you know it or not, you are a big spender, too, in your own way. Perhaps in your career you are busy helping others, be it colleagues or those to whom you direct your help. Perhaps also you give most of your time and energy to help friends and loved ones in many different ways. You are a big spender. At some point it will be very beneficial, no matter what kind of life trauma you may be dealing with, to spend a little time with those up in heaven who are channeling healing, helpful, spiritual energy to you to assist you in any way possible. This healing energy can, of course, help with your own physical health and well being, help in your relationships with others, or in many different ways. The main thing is, they're there to help you. And you and I both need to "spend a little time" tuning into the energy from the higher beings up above, allowing the divine, sacred light and energy into our beings which we can channel to meet our goals of improvement. Spend a little time, dear reader, and we can both be big spenders and big receivers of the spiritual sort.

Chapter Three
Darktown Strutter's Ball

When I received the next message once again I simply heard a voice in my head and heart. The message was the lyrics of an old song which was popular long ago known as "The Darktown Strutter's Ball." It was a song, of course, of Mama's generation. So my hunch is that the message was in fact from her, or from a wonderful guardian angel of her generation. And this time they did not change the wording on me. The lyrics which came to me were:

"I'll be down to get you in a taxi, honey
You'd better be ready around half-past eight
Now, dearie, don't be late, I want to be there when
     the band starts playing
Remember, when we get there, honey
Two steps, I'm gonna have them all
We're gonna dance off both our shoes, when they
     play the Jellyroll Blues,
Tomorrow night, at Darktown Strutter's Ball"

No words were changed, dear reader (as they say on some TV detective shows: no words were changed to protect the innocent!) No words were changed in this message, but the message came through very clearly. And the message that I received, which would also be appropriate to whatever ups and downs of life you may be going through are as follows. We'll take it one line at a time —

"I'll be down to get you in a taxi, honey"

This means to me that again our guardian angels, our Master Teachers are up in heaven waiting for us to be ready. They're coming around to get us in a taxi, or they're sending their energy to us and so we better be ready (about half past eight!). We better be ready and open the door of our physical body, our etheric body, our astral bodies to be picked up, in other words to be helped by the sacred, divine pure Light, healing energy coming around to get us in a taxi, honey. The word honey of course indicates how very much love our guardian angels, or our Master Teachers are sending to us. They feel so closely connected to us. So dear reader, again to the next line, "Now dearie don't be late." Really open the door to your self to allow the healing energy not just to surround you, but to fill up every cell and chakra of your body or every cell of the traumatic event that you may be dealing with.

The next line, dear reader,

"I want to be there when the band starts, playing"

Again meaning they're telling us we've got to be there. We've got be ready for them when their healing band starts playing for us. It's not going to be every second of every day and night, but they're up there ready to send healing energy to the place where our body, or emotional selves, or our relationships, or whatever, can take in the healing mystical, magical, significant spiritual music that they're sending down to us. Next line dear reader,

"Remember when we get there, honey"

Meaning, remember when you are ready to take in the healing either physically, mentally, emotionally or spiritually.

"Two steps we're gonna have them all"

Meaning they're going to be dancing with us. They're up there trying to do that now. Don't ever feel alone. No matter what, you're not alone, even though you may physically feel alone. Just know that they're there with you all the time. They're dancing with us whether we know it or not.

The next sentence of course is,

"We're gonna dance off both our shoes"

Again many of the messages I received were about dancing because they're trying to help me know that my equilibrium is definitely going to come back. They let me know that it probably would not be immediate. Of course I have come to know over time it certainly was not. One thing that I have learned from all this health trauma is patience, but eventually, when I'm dancing with the spiritual beings up there, we are going to dance off both our shoes, and so are you dear reader.

With your guardian angels or Master Teachers you're definitely gonna dance off both your shoes when they play the Jelly Roll Blues, tomorrow night at the Dark Town Strutter's Ball. This means to me that even though the days and nights may be dark for you, they're there for you, dancing with you and they're gonna dance off both your shoes, in a good healthy positive mental, emotional, spiritually healing way. It may take awhile. It make take until tomorrow night even though you want it to be "pronto, Tonto." But you will learn patience, and you will learn to evolve toward health and improvement.

Whatever you're going through, it will happen, even if the hour and day is dark. They're there to dance with you. They're there to pick you up in a taxi, honey. Don't be late, dear reader. They want to be there when the band starts playing, or when the healing begins to be sent to you. And don't worry, two steps you're gonna have them all.

22

Chapter Four
Angel of the Morning

As I have mentioned previously, the messages that I received were primarily in the lyrics of a song. Since I was very familiar with musicals and songs all my life because of my mother's hobby, it made good sense that they would make every effort to reach me in this way because I would actually pay attention. I'm sure they may be sending me, as well as you, dear reader, other messages in many ways that we don't take in or pay attention to. This way I could actually hear the song, even if it was simply one line, or perhaps the entire chorus, or sometimes the entire song.

A voice came to me as I was waking up in the morning and it said, "Just call me angel of the morning, angel." Clearly, the sweet voice singing the song to me was one of my guardian angels. By the way, my guardian angels, very much like yours, dear reader, have fabulous voices! And they certainly know how to stay on key and carry a tune! They also certainly know how to send wonderful healing, fabulous spiritual messages.

So, I now knew enough to refer to the angel that seemed to be singing to me many mornings as Angel of the Morning, rather than the Archangel Michael or something such as that. And of course it seems appropriate that they should try to reach us at this time of day when we're just waking up from a deep, intense sleep. Perhaps we've been dreaming of our time in heaven, or time with a lost loved one, or our lives currently, or in the future. We're just waking up to our day-to-day activities and we are about to carpe diem, or seize the day. We're wiping the sleep from our eyes and moving from the astral plane where we spent our nights in dreams and out-of-body experiences, and so on, to the daily day-to-day earth plane here. They often reach out to us while our attention is still focused inward, rather than outward, filled with work and some daily agenda of what needs to be done today and so on.

They take advantage of this little lull in our brain, soul and heart activity to really get the message across. It is often at this time of serenity, before we carpe diem, that they seem to arrive and sing to us, or perhaps in your case, it is read poetry or read from a line of scripture, or a line from a famous novel that you may know. These sweet, darling guardian angels or Master Teachers seem to reach us in many different ways, depending on what our interests are, or our hobbies or things that we know very well.

Thinking of this whole issue reminds me of when I was a little girl. As I mentioned in my earlier book, *Memories, My Parents the Mystics*, my sweet Mama, when I was just a tiny little thing, would send me to bed and tuck me in, kiss me goodnight and sing a little lullaby. The main lullaby that she sang was a song called *You Are My Sunshine*. A few of the lyrics from that song are,

"You are my sunshine, my only sunshine
You make me happy when skies are grey
You'll never know, dear, how much I love you
Please don't take my sunshine away"

Although that song never came to me as a message, I still often think of it. When I hear it, I think of sweet Mama just lulling me to sleep. She was simply helping my serenity. But the line "You are my sunshine" makes me think of all of us, dear reader. You are somebody's sunshine, whether they are on this earth plane, up in heaven, or sitting next to you on the couch. You <u>are</u> someone's sunshine, for sure.

And when this message came across to me, "Just call me angel of the morning, angel," clearly they were helping me take this ragged body of mine from a long night's journey into dawn. And, yes, they are my sunshine. So is my Mama. My wonderful sunshine. And so is everyone that I love and adore.

Please don't ever forget — your Angel of the Morning is waiting to welcome you into the dawn of a new day within you and around you. In some ways I feel like we are all angels in training here on this earth plane. So, just call them Angels of the Morning, dear angel-in-training. And remember, you are someone's fabulous sunshine.

Chapter Five
Bald Eagle

One morning a male voice came into my head. The voice said, "Chippewa, Chippewa, Chippewa." I had no idea what Chippewa meant. I was sort of squinting my eyes together and thinking, "What? Gee, what could that mean, Chippewa? Does that mean 'chip off the old block?' or something like that?" But again, they just kept saying "Chippewa, Chippewa." Finally, a voice said to me, "The tribe has renamed you Bald Eagle, wear the name with pride." What I received from that message was, "Tribe, tribe. Oh! Maybe Chippewa is a Native American Indian tribe. I never heard of that."

Now, you should know that I really love Native American Indian artwork, pow-wows, spirituality and things such as that. I think several things about myself in terms of a past life such as, I believe I was a Union soldier in the Civil War. I know that I must have been a Native American Indian in a past life because I am so interested in the Native American Indian thinking, and the ways that they used to live on this wonderful Mother Earth of ours. But, I always thought that probably I was a Navajo, Cherokee, or Apache.

After I got up that morning I kept thinking, "Chippewa, ah..." I went to a book that listed the Native American Indian tribes and the areas where they were located centuries ago in North America. I found, to my surprise, that the Chippewa <u>was</u> a tribe, part of what's called the Ojibwa Indian tribe, that was located basically around Ohio, and so on.

Interestingly, I grew up with my Dad often jokingly saying things like, "Well, I learned such and such whilst living amongst the Ojibwas." Because my Dad was born in northern Indiana, raised there and in Ohio, he learned about the Native American Indian tribes that had lived there previously. He learned about their spirituality, their culture and so on. Dad often expressed a great deal of respect for what he had learned about the Native American Indian culture. After receiving this message, of course I immediately told my Dad, and he said, "Well, gee, I guess I was living amongst the Ojibwa without knowing it!" And he and I both laughed. So, apparently I had been a member of the Chippewa tribe in a past life. To get the message that "the tribe has now renamed me Bald Eagle, wear the name with pride," <u>does</u> fill me with pride, pleasure, joy and everything else.

The fact is, when going through chemotherapy, as is typical, I did lose all my hair. So, in fact, I certainly was bald for quite awhile. In many ways the renaming of me as Bald Eagle certainly fits. The way I think of an eagle really describes a beautiful being with courage. If I was receiving the message clearly enough, it was indicating to me that they felt I had courage, even though I had become bald and I had to go through such a traumatic health experience. Receiving this message helped me feel more proud of my courage and of being able to make it through. It also raised my self-confidence a great deal to feel like, "Oh gee, the Beings up there in heaven really take into account what we're trying to do down here. They are really helping us by supporting, by loving, and by building up our self confidence as we meet the difficulties of day-to-day life."

So, just know that while the tribe up in heaven is now naming me Bald Eagle, they are also naming you something, because, no doubt, they think highly of you. They love you and they're really working to help heal you, guide you, to help you deal with the day-to-day struggles that you are facing as you go forward. Whether you know it or not, no doubt they hold you in high regard and they keep working with you to keep on going. I'm a real good Bald Eagle, or at least I try to be. And, let me just say, even though I was bald for awhile, I went through that phase and now I'm not bald any more. Thank goodness! But I am trying to fly high, to keep on going, and I know you can too, dear reader.

Chapter Six
Rainy Day People

The next message that I received, was a few lines from a song called, *Rainy Day People*. Their meaning was clear enough:

> "Rainy day people don't lie when they tell 'ya
> they've been down there too
> Rainy day people don't mind if you cry a tear
> or two"

And,

> "Rainy day people all know there's no sorrow they can't rise above"

So, in some ways, dear reader, I guess I'm a rainy day person, and, chances are, so are you. No doubt we don't think of ourselves this way, of course. But, as the song says, "Rainy day people all know there's no sorrow they can't rise above." So, believe in yourself. There's no sorrow, there's no difficulty, there's no trauma that you can't rise above.

And when I think of the line,

"Rainy day people don't lie when they tell you they've been down there too"

I think about the importance of people who love you, and will support your emotional ups and downs. Often the people around you don't lie to you when they say, they've been down experiencing really, really tough stuff as well in their lives. But they are there to help and support you. And so are your guardian angels and Master Teachers.

Sometimes it is easy to feel, that you're the only person that has been through whatever, and that no one else can really understand the depth of your depression, your misery, your sadness, your difficulty and so on. There are people, guardian angels and Divine Beings upstairs that do understand it, and that did go through something similar. They seemed to take that sorrow and rise above. And you can, too. But just know that you are not alone where you are. Other people, and other Divine Beings, have been there, and are there with you. They are really, really working to support you, to take you by the hand, to walk you along, to help you in any way possible. They're there with you. I thank goodness that I was not alone.

And the next line, as you know, is,

"Rainy day people don't mind if you cry a tear or two"

Please know that it is perfectly acceptable and also really, really good that you express your feelings. You may cry, be sad, be depressed, need the help of a really good therapist and some really good friends around you. They put their arms around you when you cry and hold you close. Because that's often the way that we can get through all this.

It's not only okay if you cry a tear or two, but it's also really smart. It helps unburden you. It helps to let go of what you've just been dealing with, and acknowledge the feelings that you have. There's nothing wrong with crying, with being sad. But know that you can walk through it, and let it go. Unburden yourself and keep going. Feel free to cry a tear or two, dear reader. Express your feelings. Feel them, process them, talk about them with friends and/or with a good therapist. Know that you're not alone.

There's no sorrow that you can't rise above. And once you do believe it, believe in yourself and know that you are not alone. Ask for help from those around you. Even though you will be a rainy day person, you will also look ahead and be moving into the blue skies smiling at you. And soon, nothing but blue skies will you see! And when you come into a blue sky section of your spiritual evolution, you will then be able to look over your shoulder, reach back and help a rainy day person going through a severe storm.

Chapter Seven
Don't Sleep

The seventh message I received came about a month after the previous one. It was the line from the Woody Allen movie, *Bullets Over Broadway*. The line in the movie is actually,

"Don't speak."

One character is lovingly turning toward another, putting her fingers up to their lips and saying, "Don't speak, don't speak." This is said in a loving, joking way.

However, what I heard from a Master Teacher or guardian angel was a voice saying,

"Don't sleep, don't sleep."

Of course, dear reader, it did not mean to keep myself awake 24/7. It meant don't let the inner soul part of me sleep. The messages urged me to not let myself become a couch potato. I had to make sure that I didn't simply get up, go downstairs, and sit there watching TV all day. The message that I received meant, "Keep working, Sita. We're here to help you. We love you. We do not want your soul, your body, your mental savvy, or your emotions to sleep." They meant sleep in the form of, don't just lie there passively. Try to keep active. Try to allow the Healing, Pure, Sacred, Divine, Loving Light to pour down upon you, to surround you, and then take it fully into your body. Don't sleep. Don't turn away from what is being sent to you for help.

So, dear reader, the message that I feel I received, and my suggestion to you is, don't simply let other people, or Divine Beings do all of the work for you. I'm sure you wouldn't do this anyway. But don't simply sleep. Don't be passive, or become a couch potato. Really, really work, and keep moving so that you can continue evolving spiritually. Keep healing and learning from the trauma which has just occurred in your life. Don't sleep. And, of course, the guardian angels, or the Master Teachers, or both are saying this to you in loving ways.

Don't sleep. Keep walking. Keep chugging. Keep working and opening up to let in the pure Sacred, Divine energy that is coming to you. Take it in and keep moving forward down the path of life that you are on.

As I said previously, of course this message is meant metaphorically. It is really important, healing and helpful for you to get some sleep every evening. But don't allow your mind, your body or your soul to go to sleep without really taking full advantage of the wonderful helping hands that try to reach you. Divine Hands that try to pick you up and help you along the way. Keep plugging along. You've got a lot of helpers out there loving you, saying "Don't sleep."

Chapter Eight
The Rose

This morning when I was working out at my physical therapy to which I go for one hour everyday to help me deal with my loss of equilibrium from the brain tumor, I received a message no doubt from one of my guardian angels. I'm telling you this, dear reader, because I often feel that I am a messenger and the divine messages that come to me are no doubt meant as a help to me, but mainly are meant to go through me to you to assist with whatever trauma you may be dealing with in your life at present.

My physical therapist was challenging me to walk from one end of the room to the other without my walker or cane, simply wearing my leg brace. She, of course, would be there to protect me from falling every step of the way. However, I felt a great deal of fear because I have fallen before and it's hard for me to take risks at this point in my recovery.

As you may have experienced the emotion of fear has a way of penetrating our bodies, and when the fear is unnecessary it has a way of limiting us, no matter what our goals are in life. I'm not only talking about physical health issues, but inappropriate fear can affect one's healing processes, one's relationships, one's experiences at work, or any of our other life issues.

As the physical therapist was standing there waiting for me to dare take that first step, this wonderful song that I have not hear of, nor thought of in years came to me. This song is called "The Rose" and was made famous by Bette Midler. The part of the lyrics that came to me were as follows:

"It's the heart afraid of breaking
    that never learns to dance
It's the dream afraid of waking
    that never takes the chance
It's the one who won't be taken
    who cannot seem to give
And the soul afraid of dyin'
    that never learns to live

When the night has been too lonely
    and the road has been too long
And you think that love is only
    for the lucky and the strong
Just remember in the winter
    far beneath the winter snows
Lies the seed that with the sun's love
    in the Spring becomes the Rose."

As I have said before, this wonderful message from On High was sent by my Master Teachers or guardian angels to convey the message that I was allowing fear to restrict my recovery. Of course, the recovery process does take practice, no matter what you are recovering from, but it is always good and important to keep taking that next step toward life improvement and toward spiritual growth no matter what that goal may be in your life. Please do not allow fear to limit your growth. Of course, I'm not suggesting that you'll need to go sky diving with a parachute, but do keep walking down that healing, spiritual path even when there is darkness and fear around you. Believe me, your guardian angel is there to help you every step of the way.

No doubt at some point in your life you will feel that the night has been too lonely, and the road has been too long, but please do not let yourself think that the divine healing process is only for the lucky and the strong. You have the Divine Light around and within you, and as you continue to let that Divine Light in, that seed that is the core of you becomes the Rose.

Chapter Nine
Storm the Bastille

The next message that I received was very simple and very short. There were just three words, "Storm the Bastille." This referred, of course to the French Revolution. But I took it to mean, and what I'm sure they were telling me, to storm your own Bastille. In other words, to take over your own body, your own life. Use the control you have. Not for manipulation, and terrible control over other people. But the control that you have over your own physical body, your own spiritual growth and understanding, and your own life. Storm your own Bastille, dear reader. In other words take over your self. Or, as people sometimes say, "Wake up and smell the roses."

We can, of course, storm our own Bastille in many ways. These ways include:

- turning to friends for help
- getting a good therapist
- going to the gym to work out to make ourselves stronger
- to storm the Bastille of our bodies, and/or, really eating more nutritious foods rather than simply very quick fast food at the local fast food take-out place on the corner.

And there are many, many ways that you can storm the Bastille of your body.

Also, you can storm the Bastille of your emotional body by using, as I have said, good friends, good therapists or perhaps meditating. Go inside, look what's there, feel it, take it in. Once you spend a little bit of time in your inner Bastille, sending your focus inward to your own sweet heart and emotional self, you also can ask your Master Teachers, guardian angels and loved ones upstairs to send you down healing, Sacred Divine Light Energy and Power. You're much more likely to receive it, of course, during the time you are storming your emotional Bastille.

You could also storm your mental Bastille by doing such things as reading a good book, whether it is just casual reading or spiritual reading, for example. Or perhaps attending a spiritual conference. You can find your self growing spiritually, storming your own spiritual Bastille.

You can meet the challenges that surround you. You don't have to simply look at yourself from a distance, like you're sitting in an ivory tower far away. There you are just doing nothing but work, going home, then going back to work, and then going back home. Really living sort of a nothing existence. Don't look at yourself that way and just accept it.

Storm the Bastille, dear reader. You can do it. You've got control over that. Control over your physical, emotional, mental, and your spiritual body.

Storm your Bastille. And, of course, storm it in a good way. I'm not suggesting that you wreak violence on your self in some way. Let in the Divine Light that surrounds you. Let the Sacred Divine Power and Energy into your own life in many different ways. In doing such as that, you are storming your own Bastille.

That Sacred Divine Light, Power, Energy simply is waiting for you to open up the door. Open it up more widely, dear reader. You can do that. And there are many different ways to do it. But just know that you've got your own Bastille which you can storm as well. Bring a flower or two along with you while you're storming . In other words, create your own inner self with joy, love, compassion, healing. Bring it in with you, to carry you forward all along the path.

Chapter Ten
Dancing in the Dark

Most of the messages which I received over this time were primarily about walking or dancing. This helped me know that I could get back my old equilibrium, which was ruined by the radiation damage. They were telling me that, with their help and with my determination, I could simply refuse to sit on the couch and accept what had happened to me as the end of the story. They kept informing me through their messages that I had to do what I could, and that they were up there doing all they could do to heal me totally.

And again, sometimes they changed a word or two on me to help me know that it was a divine message, not simply something that illuminated in my brain suddenly. For example, instead of the phrase, "Waddya talk?" which is sometimes what one person says to another person, meaning, "What the heck are you talking about?" What I received was the word, "Whaddya walk?" meaning "Walk, Sita. You can walk. You can walk down the spiritual path. You can walk through the terror of health crisis. Determindly walk into health, and let the divine light guide you. Whaddya walk? Talk the talk *and* walk the walk, don't just talk the talk." Upon hearing this message, I dashed to the local sporting goods store and bought a treadmill so that I could walk the walk. I often use the treadmill for, as the British say, a morning constitutional, an afternoon constitutional, and an evening constitutional. I wanted to do my share of the walking, as they were up there doing their share of helping me, guiding me, strengthening me, doing the waddya walk.

Also at this time, some lines from the famous Bruce Springsteen song, *Dancing In the Dark* came to me. This time they did not change a word or two, but let me get the full extent of the song. Also they showed me the meaning in terms of me. The following are the lyrics of the song that came to me. And after the lyrics I will tell you the meaning that I construed from receiving them:

"You can't start a fire, you can't start a fire without
   a spark
This gun's for hire even if we're just dancing in the
   dark
Message keeps getting clearer, radio's on and I'm
   moving 'round the place
I check my look in the mirror, I wanna change my
   clothes, my hair, my face
Man, I ain't gettin' nowhere just sitting in a dump
   like this
There's somethin' happening somewhere, baby, I
   just know that there is

You can't start a fire, you can't start a fire without
   a spark
This gun's for hire, even if we're just dancing in
   the dark"

The meaning that I received from this wonderful, fabulous, danceable song which I love, was as follows:

When they say you can't start a fire without a spark, what they meant in terms of this situation was, "Sita you can't become healed totally without lending your effort to it." They need a spark down here because there's a divine fire, an essence and a fabulous healing energy coming down to me. But it can't reach me without my lighting the Divine Light within me, the divine spark. So again, I couldn't just sit on the couch. I had to get up, meditate, go to physical therapy, get on my treadmill, get on the stationary bike, use an ab machine, really build my center and start walking around more efficiently. But they couldn't help guide me without the spark coming from me. I had to open myself up to receive the Sacred Divine White Light, Fire, Energy, Power and Healing coming down to me. Thus, they were saying that they couldn't start the fire within me without a spark coming from me. This single line, "Message keeps getting clearer," could not be clearer to me. Again, their messages were becoming clearer.

"Radio's on and I'm moving 'round the place"

In other words, they were reminding me there's healing in music. There can be. It's good to use that essence, that energy to really go inside and help heal your mind, body and spirit. Radio is on and start moving around the place, Sita, don't just sit there. Also, there was a time when I looked in the mirror and I could not stand what I saw. I could not stand it that my hair, face and clothing were not the way that they used to be.

So again,

"I check my look in the mirror, I wanna change my clothes, my hair, my face"

And of course I was able to do that with divine guidance and help.

I needed to change the way I looked. I didn't mean to go simply without being able to wash my hair. I can get my hair washed at a beauty salon. I could change the clothes, not simply wearing sweatshirts and pants with no color in them, but add some vitality. They didn't have to become uncomfortable, but simply more colorful, vibrant, more filled with health and healing that I could draw into myself. With divine help, I could change my clothes, my hair, my face.

The next line, of course,

"Man I ain't gettin' nowhere just living in a dump like this"

That is the way I felt about the way I looked, and the turn that my life had taken. But I didn't have to live in a dump like that.

"There's somethin' happening somewhere, baby, I just know that there is"

Well, dear reader, there *is* something happening somewhere, and I just know that there is. What's happening somewhere is happening within us, being guided down from the heavens above us. Divinely, sacredly, purely. We have to open ourselves up to receive it, and then send it out into our lives. Remember, dear reader, you cannot start a fire without a spark. Start that spark within you, and accept the Sacred Energy coming down to you. It is that fire, added to your divine spark, your divine light, that will emerge as total healing to keep guiding you forward.

Make that, let's call it a divine gun within you, for hire. For hire in this case meaning to turn it over to the Divine Essence that is coming to you. You've got a sacred gun within you. Use it for hire. Ask for guidance from the divine ones that are around you. Guidance to help light your way. Even if you're just dancing in the dark, you can dance your way into the divine spiritual light, guiding you further down your spiritual path.

Chapter Eleven
Confidence Stone

The next message I received came to me as a result of a little gift that my Dad had brought me from his Astara spiritual trip to Egypt. Just about every spiritual tour that he took, bless his heart, he would bring back little gifts for me. It was so nice to have little things from whatever country to which my father had gone. And often, of course, in years past, when I went with him on the Astara spiritual trips, I bought a thing or two myself. But in this case, of course, I could not go because I was just going through treatment, and starting my recovery process. He brought back from Astara's spiritual tour of Egypt a little stone in a carrying case. The stone itself had a paper explanation about what the stone was meant for. The paper said that it was a "confidence stone." I had placed the little stone on a table that one could see when first entering the door of my apartment. I placed the little paper explanation there also.

Months after I had first received it from my Dad, I was just looking at it, and hoping that it would help me build my confidence. Holding it up to my heart, another message came through. And, lo and behold, it was, of course, a song about confidence from the wonderful movie, *Sound of Music*. The lines that I received were part of the song.

"I have confidence in sunshine
I have confidence in rain
I have confidence in spring time
Besides which, you see, I have confidence in me
Strength doesn't lie in numbers, strength doesn't lie in wealth"

The ending lines of the song came through to me even more loudly, powerfully and with a great deal of emphasis.

"Strength lies in nights of peaceful slumber
When you wake up, wake up, you're healthy!"

Of course, when I heard that line I just smiled. I felt that my wonderful guardian angels, Master Teachers and sweet Mama were trying to tell me,

"Wake up, wake up, Sita, you are healthy."

In other words to me what they were saying is, "Don't just sleep all day long. Don't just be busy running to the bathroom with nausea, and things like that. Yes, all that is part of the healing process because of the terrible treatment that you've had to go through. However, it is important that you really wake up, not just your consciousness, but wake up your spirit, wake up your body, wake up everything. You have to begin physical therapy because you are healthy." I really believe that is what they were trying to tell me — "Wake up, wake up, you are healthy." I felt I had to say to myself, "Okay, I get it, I'm healthy. I really have to make the most of whatever time I have left here on this wonderful Mother Earth of ours."

And so, months after it was given, this sweet confidence stone brought to me a wonderful message. Yes, I was in peaceful slumber. In some ways it wasn't so peaceful, of course. I had really disassociated my mind from the dreadful treatment that I had to go through. But even though, basically, I slumbered in some way, it was time for me to wake up, wake up. I had to do everything that I could with physical therapy and different forms of alternative, new age healing to really, really get going with my life.

You, of course, dear reader, whether you know it or not, have the confidence song within your heart and soul, as well. You may be going through a health trauma, or any of the ups and downs of life in terms of troubled relationships with loved ones, a dreadful work situation, the terrible process of seeing someone whom you love who may not be doing very well health wise. Whatever you may be going through, you can wake up. Wake yourself up from the terrible downturn that you are going through, or have been through. And how to do this? Perhaps wake up by your own physical therapy, or seeing a good psychotherapist. Perhaps by not only seeing simply a

Western medical doctor, but adding an Eastern alternative medical doctor, and different forms of healing so that you are getting the best of both worlds.

Talk to friends and loved ones about whatever you may be going through. Bring into your life something that will give you the confidence that you need. Do something that can raise your own self esteem, bring you joy, bring you health, bring you happiness. Become active, dear reader, in meeting your own inner needs, whatever they may be. Build up that confidence, that self-esteem. That love of self can and should radiate, out to others around us. I, of course, do not mean, dear reader, become narcissistic. I mean really build up your heart, your spirit, your soul, your body in some way that brings you confidence in *you*. Because you're healthy, or can become more healthy as you go along the way. It is important that you carry with you that confidence, that self-esteem, or respect and self regard that will help you continue through the days and nights ahead, and get even better as you go forth.

I can't thank my Dad enough for the wonderful confidence stone that he brought to me. Yes, I do have confidence in sunshine, rain and spring time, and our wonderful Mother Earth. And, I really, really want us to work on building up her confidence enough, so that we as human beings are not just trampling upon her. But we also need to remember that our strength does not lie in wealth, but in that fact that we can do it. We can build our own self-respect, self confidence to get to where we want to go.

I would suggest that on your home altar, or bureau, you put some small, little trinket that will remind you of the confidence within you. Something that signifies this for you. It could be anything that you like. A gong, perhaps. Or a sacred candle representing the eternal flame of spiritual growth. Or a statue of the Buddha, Kwan-Yin, Mother Mary, Goddess-Priestess Isis, or any Master Teacher. Whatever would help you feel confident within your own self, and confident in your spiritual progress along the way.

Keep moving, dear reader. You can do it. If I could, my hunch is that you can.

Chapter Twelve
Key Largo

The next message I received was something similar to a famous line from a classic movie. The movie I'm talking about is *Key Largo,* starring Lauren Becall and Humphrey Bogart. And, this time my wonderful guardian angels and Master Teachers changed a word or two on me so that I would know for sure it was a message from above. I was simply thinking about working as hard as I could to improve my walking, and to get my equilibrium back.

Suddenly, into my mind came an image of wonderful Lauren Becall heading to the doorway, and turning around at the open door. Calling back to Humphrey Bogart, she said the famous line,

"You know how to whistle, don't you, Steve? You just put you lips together and blow."

The actual line that I received from heaven was,

"You know how to walk, don't you Sita? Just put your legs together and walk."

The message, of course, conveys both the simplicity of the goal that I was trying to reach and, the difficulty.

Easier said than done, as they say. It reminded me of something that Jesus said in one of the scriptures where's he's working on healing people. When Jesus put his hand out to a crippled man he said, "Pick up thy bed and walk." Now, giving someone the power to walk is absolutely miraculous, of course. But also saying, "Pick up thy bed" to me refers to a great deal of the healing process that you have to go through. It's not simply that suddenly everything is back to normal, and off you go dancing down the street.

"Pick up thy bed" — how difficult could that have been for someone, especially at that time? Just think, if today some Master Teacher said that to you. Imagine if you had to somehow tuck your mattress under your arm to walk down the street. It's awfully hard, but somehow you're channeled the wonderful, diving healing energy to enable you to do just that. You have to do your own part of it. You have to pick up thy bed, and learn how to walk once again.

Again, I received the message that they're up there doing everything they can to help me. They reminded me that I know how to walk. I had it in me. They were sending healing energy down to me. I had to put my legs together and walk to the nearest physical therapist's place, and do all that I could to get my equilibrium back.

Sounds simple, dear reader? Believe me, it is not. But, we all have the ability within us to walk further down our spiritual paths, no matter what's in our way. Put your mind to it, dear reader. Put your heart to it, whatever your goal may be. You can do it. Just put your mind and heart together, your consciousness, and your spirit. Walk. You will have divine guidance every step of the way, from Jesus, from Mother Mary, from Buddha, from Moses, from the Goddess-Priestess Isis, from many who are up there attempting to guide you along.

Chapter Thirteen
It's Been a Long, Long Time

Well, once again, it was just after dawn. I had awakened and, no, I did not stick my mattress under my arm and walk towards the bathroom sink to brush my teeth! However, while I was in the bathroom brushing my teeth, I happened to glance at myself in the mirror to see how I was looking at that point in my healing process.

Suddenly, once again, a message came to me. The message was some lyrics from an old, old song, and this time no words were changed at all. However, as has happened before, it was a song I had not thought of, nor had I heard in many, many, years. The song title I believe is, *It's Been A Long, Long Time*. As I heard this song in my head come out of nowhere, I knew that it had to be Mama, sending me this wonderful message. She was reminding me that I was getting well. Yes, it had been a long, long time, but I was getting back to normal, and back to something akin to how I used to look.

The message is as follows:

"Kiss me once, then kiss me twice
Then kiss me once again
It's been a long, long time

Haven't felt like this, my dear
Since can't remember when
It's been a long, long time"

And, yes, it had been a long, long, awful time since I felt like that. I felt a little bit back to my old self. I put my fingers to my lips and gave a kiss up to heaven, thanking my Mom, my guardian angels and Master Teachers that have helped me along the healing process. And there is a long process still to go, of course. But they reminded me that, yes, it had been a long time. I was feeling more like myself again, thank God, and I could keep going. And they are helping me go every step of the way. You, too, can return, dear reader, to something like you used to feel and even much, much better.

The spiritual path often, I believe, swirls its way around to bring us back to the same sort of event. I believe it spirals up, and we come around to find the same sort of issues meeting us again. Just as your life has spiraled up, your spiritual knowledge has spiraled up, and your place along the spiritual path has spiraled up. So you may well find yourself back in the same place, but responding in very different ways.

Why, dear reader? Because you're wiser. Not just from life experience, but from spiritual experience, and spiritual lessons that you've taken into yourself. Yes, you could say to yourself something like, "Haven't felt like this, dear reader, since can't remember when." It's been a long, long time, but, chances are, you're even better than you were before.

66

Chapter Fourteen
Michael, Row the Boat Ashore

The next message that came to me was, as usual, to the tune of an old song. But, again, the sweet Master Teachers and guardian angels changed some wording on me so that I could really, really know that I was receiving the message from above. The song was, "Michael Row the Boat Ashore." And, of course, the original lyrics are as follows:

"Michael row the boat ashore, hallelujah
Michael row the boat ashore, hallelujah..."

What came to me was the following:

"Michael roll away the stone, hallelujah
Michael roll away the stone, hallelujah"

And, again, the message I received from this was basically, "Yes, Sita, you are well. You can go back to your life. The stone has been rolled away from the cave of terrible health trauma that you have been in." Again, the Biblical significance of perhaps the Archangel Michael rolling away the stone, hallelujah, to help me get up and go on with my life. So, please know that you have guardian angels around you, Master Teachers over you and wonderful archangels, as well, no matter what religion you belong to, to help you roll away the stone which is blocking your own life. Be it a health crisis, or a crisis of some other sort, your stone can and will be rolled away for you. Michael, Buddha, Goddess-Priestess Isis, or whomever, can roll away that stone for you, and help you come out of the cave to continue moving down your own spiritual path.

This message was simply to let me know that they are there for me, and there for you, also. No matter what you may be having such terrible difficulty with, they are there to help you roll away the stone which is blocking your progress, and your life. Work with your guardian angels to roll away the stone for you, dear reader. You can do it.

Along about the same time, a similar message came to me, although, of course, the song and the generation from which it came was very, very different. This time, it was a line from a famous Bob Seeger song. And the line that came to me was,

"Like a rock, charging from a gate"

You can charge from the gate that may be holding you back, dear reader, particularly if you have a very good, strong foundation under you. It could be a strong foundation of simple physical exercise, which is very, very important to keep charging from that gate, and/or it could be needed counseling or therapy. Perhaps you could use help from loved ones, friends, family or spiritual help from meditation, yoga, reading spiritual books, or attending spiritual conferences. You can charge from the gate that may be holding you back no matter what. Your guardian angels are up there to help you with the charging forward.

Chapter Fifteen
Physician, Heal Thyself

Well, I was beginning to understand the old adage, "Physician, heal thyself."

Of course, this does not mean to be closed to accepting Western medical care. This can be very, very useful and helpful in every which way. However, it is important to know that we, ourselves, can be of assistance in the healing process, and get assistance from what is known as Eastern or alternative health care. I'm referring to healing such as, for example, acupuncture, chiropractic, Reiki, crano-sacral healing, neuro feedback, and so on. In addition to all of these things, you can be of help to yourself. You are a physician, dear reader. You can help heal yourself.

I, of course, received this message more clearly than I had wanted or intended. But I now understand much more depthfully the phrase, "Physician heal thyself." Along, of course, with a wonderful support group, both Eastern and Western.

Around this time another traditional message came to me which is:

"Now is the time for all good men to come to the aid of their country."

The message I received added several words, here and there. It was as follows:

There comes a time for all good men and women to come to the aid of themselves.

This wonderful message, of course, helped clarify and intensify the old adage for me of "Physician heal thyself." Come to the aid of yourself. Yes, of course, others can be there to aid you. You may well need them very, very much, no matter what you're going through. Again, it could be a health, emotional, relationship, or work-oriented crisis. Any kind of crisis that you may be attempting to go through, and recover from. But you, dear reader, can step up to the plate and help with your healing process. There does come a time for all good men and women to come to the aid of themselves.

But I do not mean to indicate that you should brush other people aside, regardless. It is good, dear reader, to create you own inner circle of friends, loved ones and professional helpers, whomever they may be. I suggest that you create an inner circle of people whom you admire, respect and think of highly. They can be of great help to you as you proceed down your path to assist yourself. But, of course, with them helping you, you need to be of help to them for you.

Chapter Sixteen
Starry Starry Night

The next message that I received was a lot more than simply one or two lines of a song. It was quite a bit of the song. It was not a song from the 30's, 40's or 50's. It's a song about the wonderful artist, Vincent Van Gogh. I will tell you the lines of the song as they are sung, but they did change this one word for me, and I will make that clear. I will then let you know what interpretation I made of the change in wording. The part of the song that came to me is as follows:

"And how you suffered for your sanity
And how you tried to set them free
They would not listen
They did not know how
Perhaps they'll listen now
For they could not love you
But still your love was true
And when no hope was left in sight
On that starry, starry night
You took you life as lovers often do
But I could have told you, Vincent
This world was never meant for one as beautiful
    as you"

The actual message which I received, dear reader, was a simple change in one word of the line before the very last line:

"But I could have told you, Memphis
This world was never meant for one as beautiful
    as you"

I should let you know Memphis is the name of a very, very sweet grey cat that belongs to someone very dear to me. I called the cat's owner that very night to make sure that Memphis was okay. I thought perhaps I was picking up something to tell me that Memphis was not well. But that was not the case. Memphis was just fine. So, I asked for guidance. Why did they send me this part of the song? And why did they change that one word? And then, all of a sudden, it seemed to become very, very clear to me.

Thank goodness Memphis was fine. In fact, dear reader, the message was telling me that I should use that cat-like part of me, the sweet Memphis that is in me to do the cross crawl, to help myself gain my equilibrium and balance back. Not across the floor, of course. But to really get to using the cross crawl on let's say a treadmill, a glider or a stationary bike that's arms also move so that I could reignite the proper nerves, muscles and the part of my brain that can do the cat-like sort of cross crawl. This way of exercising, which I began right I after I received that message, has proven to be very, very helpful to me.

The cross crawl, has been so important in helping to learn to move forward one arm with the opposite leg, and the then one leg with the opposite arm. As I say, they were telling me to use that cat-like part of myself. In many ways, dear reader, we all have totem animals. We all have parts of ourselves, our personality, our character, our body movement, whatever, that is very, very like certain wonderful animals out there in Sweet Mother Nature. Yes, I could do, and I did the cross crawl to help myself get stronger, and to improve my mobility.

Also they were telling me with this song to take my life and change it. Not simply accepting it for the way it was, which was terrible, but for really moving forward. Change my life, take my life, and move it down the path. Whatever trauma you may be going through, dear reader, whatever could be challenging you at the moment, I suggest that you take your life into your own hands. You can make it better. And, believe me, there is help, divine help above you and around you to help change it for the better.

Think of a totem animal for yourself. For example, I often think of my totem animals, one of which is the wolf, another is the humming bird, and also the horse. All of them have characteristics, and personalities that are similar to mine. I tend to move very quickly, and sometimes I make decisions too fast. But often the decisions that I make, rather than pondering something for years, turn out to be very good. The wolf howls at the moon, which to me means that the wolf loves Mother Nature, as do I. I love to see a full moon, or a crescent moon. I love to see trees, and be up close to them. I love to see every, every aspect of wonderful Mother Nature, and the creatures that are on this fabulous Mother Earth with us.

So, I suggest you put your trauma in your heart and hands. Look to your own totem animals. If you have not chosen any, think about the ways you move, the ways you think, the ways you feel. Consider the way you communicate with others. Think of an animal whose own inner soul is similar to yours, or who in some way personifies a part of who you are. I would suggest, dear reader, using that image of your totem animal as a way to help you change your life by improving it. You can use that image to help you get farther down the spiritual, healing path.

Chapter Seventeen
Alexander's Ragtime Band

I was simply sitting there on my couch in my apartment after eating breakfast when I received my next message. It was another one from Mama's generation, so I'm pretty well convinced that it was she that sent it to me. Suddenly, I heard in my head, my Mama's sweet voice just singing this song. The song is called, "Alexander's Ragtime Band." This time they did not change a word on me at all. But they didn't need to. The part of the song that I received is as follows:

"Come on along, come on along,
    let me take you by the hand
Up to the man, up to the man,
    whose the leader of the band
And if you want to hear *The Swanee River*
    played in ragtime
Come on and hear, come on and hear
    Alexander's Ragtime Band"

When I received this message, dear reader, I instantly thought of my wonderful Mom. She would often say the phrase, "I swan." This is a Southern term meaning something like, "I can't believe it," or, "Oh, my gosh." And, of course, it is a phrase connected with the Swanee River. "Well, I swan!" she'd say. So it was clear that the message was from her, and she was saying, "Come on along, sweetheart, don't just sit there. Let me take you to the leader of the band." In other words, in my mind, to the Mother-Father God. And, of course, I don't mean take my soul up to heaven, but "Get up, get up, sweetheart." She was saying, "Come on along, let me connect you to the divine." That was the message which I received that day. I felt she was suggesting that I work to make that connection between myself and the Divine even more solid and strong.

And, yes, I would want to hear *The Swanee River* played in ragtime. In other words, meaning something like, "My gosh, don't just sit there. My gosh, Sita, you can do better, come on." Come on along, come on along, Alexander's Ragtime Band. The best in the land, my honey lamb, my dear reader.

You've got access to the best band in the land also, no matter what land you may be in! The best band is within you, above you, and around you. Come on along. You can make your way down that path with help from above and from inside you. You're the leader of your own band. You're the leader of the best band in the land. You're your own honey lamb, in some ways, I swan!

So lift that part of you up. Let the Divine take you by the hand, and really reinforce and strengthen that connection with the Divine that you have in you already. In the strengthening of this divine connection, making it more solid, strong and clear, you will help yourself get over the trauma with which you are presently dealing. That wonderful band is there to help you.

Come on along, dear reader, take yourself by the hand. Let your totem animals, your guardian angels, your Master Teachers take you by the hand, and lead you down that path to face the challenges and get past them.

Alexander's Ragtime Band is there to help you. That band of brothers, sisters and guardian angels and Master Teachers just standing over you and guiding you along the way.

Chapter Eighteen
Start Spreading the News

Well, after I had begun vigorously working out with my physical therapist to help me regain my equilibrium and balance, I received another message from the wonderful guardian angels and Master Teachers above me. The song, of course, is literally a song about a city called *New York, New York*. But, again the way they sent the message to me was to change several words here and there to make their message very clear. The message I received was as follows:

> "Start spreading the news,
>   I'm feeling better each day
> I'll make a brand new start of it,
>   in my new body
> If I can make it there, I'll make it anywhere,
>   it's up to you body, body"

In other words, it was clear that I was coming out of my cocoon. I'm making a brand new start of my new life in my new body. Of course, there were many days, dear reader, that I longed for my old life, and my old body. I missed it. I wish this had never happened to me. However, since it did, I had to make the best of it. And, again, it was clear, if I could make it in this new body, (which is very physically challenged in ways that are totally unexpected, and that I would not wish on my worst enemy), I could make it anywhere.

And, of course, you, too, can make it through the turmoil, and trauma which you may be experiencing at present. It may mean a new body for you. You may be physically challenged, as well. Or, you may be relationship challenged, or perhaps emotionally, spiritually, or job-wise challenged. You may be economically challenged. Whatever your challenge may be, you can make it. There are wonderful guardian angels and Master Teachers up there waiting to help you.

There might come a time, of course, that, try as we might, giving it all we've got, progress stops at a certain point. It is often hard to tell what the reason for this may be. No doubt there is some reason for it, which perhaps we will find out when we make our way to heaven. One of our chief guardian angels may very likely sit down and talk to us, telling us why we had such difficulty. This wonderful guardian angel may well explain to us the spiritual significance, and the spiritual lessons we were to learn from dealing with whatever the trauma may have been. So, please, dear reader, I do not mean for a moment, that try as you might, if you do not make it to the goal it's all your fault. It is not. There may be negative karma to pay off, and/or *important* spiritual lessons to be learned for your soul growth and progress.

But I believe that, come your days in heaven and your next life in which I believe you'll find yourself even further along the spiritual ladder and in a much happier situation. Again, your efforts to make a positive, really, really important and good difference for you in this life, no matter what your trauma may be, will be of significance this very day, tomorrow, next week, next month and/or in your next lifetime. Every time you try to accomplish something, which is for your Highest Good, anything you work and pray for, will come to be eventually. You will make important, significant spiritual, emotional, mental and physical progress. You can count on it. If you can make it, dear reader, through whatever you may be going through, you can make it anywhere. And so you will.

Chapter Nineteen
Sita, Girl

I received another message from Mama recently. I had just dropped Daddy off at his house, and was driving back to my apartment at the time. Thankfully, I've become well enough to start up street driving again, but not freeway driving, yet.

At any rate, I was driving home and was alone in my car, when suddenly I heard Mother's wonderful voice in my head. The voice had a slight Southern accent, as Mama always did when she was casual at home. After all, she was from Texas. In her early career as an actress, she had learned to moderate her accent when in public in order to be considered for more roles. But at home she often spoke with a slight one.

At any rate, I heard her voice in my head say, "Sita, Girl." This, of course, is a Southern expression. If you ever used to see the TV show called *The Waltons*, they often referred to one of the kids as "John Boy." Well, my mom and all my aunts, her sisters, always called me "Sita Girl," but I haven't been referred to that way in years.

I heard her voice say, "Sita Girl," then I heard nothing more. Out loud I said, "Hi, Mom. I love you. Can you tell me more? I'm not getting the message."

And I heard her lovely Southern voice in my head again, this time saying, "You're good to go, honey." Meaning to me, "You are healthy." So I took it all in, teared up a bit, and said out loud, "Thank you, Mama. Thanks for letting me know and thanks for all the work you've done helping to heal me. And as you and Dad often said, 'I will love you 'til who laid the rail,'" meaning forever.

So, dear reader kiddo, I'm good to go and you're good to go, too, whether you know it or not. And our guardian angels, deceased loved ones and Master Teachers, are up there helping us be good to go.

Chapter Twenty
Sally at the Oscars

As I was continuing on in my healing process, at one point while I had my eyes closed during a meditation, I just happened to see the image of someone accepting an Oscar. That person was Sally Field. You may remember that very famous moment when she was accepting the Oscar and said, "You like me, you really like me." It is important to accept that teamwork and that support from your healers. Again, no matter what you're dealing with, you should have a group of cheerleaders and supporters around you on this Earth plane. If you do not have this, it's important that you bring them into your life, and into your process of moving forward. My suggestion is to get a good support team around you in some way, no matter what you're dealing with.

And yes, dear reader, to be certain, you *are* an Oscar winner for your own progress and healing. You are the winner up there on a platform saying, "You like me." Also emotionally expressing, "You love me. You heal me." You need to have, should have, and hopefully do have an important team of helpers, healers and support groups here on this plane of life and also definitely, you have a support group on the other plane of life, as well, known as heaven. Upon that higher plane of life, yes they do like you, they love you, and they are working to heal you and help you move forward. So, just like Sally Field, dear reader, no matter what you're dealing with, you will be able to stand up on a platform at some point and say, "You like me, you really like me. You love me. You heal me. Thank you, my wonderful support team." You're a fabulous Oscar winner, dear reader.

Chapter Twenty-One
I'm Melting

The next message came to me as I was worrying about the results of an upcoming MRI that I had to have. Again, during a time of meditation, as I had my eyes closed and I was attuned to my inner self, I received the words. Actually, of course, they are famous words from the movie, *The Wizard of Oz*. The wicked witch toward the end of the movie says, "I'm melting, I'm melting." I received this image and this message from above, meaning to me my illness had melted away.

And, of course, thank goodness, it was true. When I did get the results of this MRI, my illness had not totally disappeared, my brain tumor cells were still there, but they had shrunk tremendously from the treatment that I had received. My illness had melted away, dear reader. And the difficulty confronting your life can, and will melt away also. "I'm melting, I'm melting." Get help from around you and above you. And work to make whatever difficulty you're dealing with melt away.

Chapter Twenty-Two
The Boxer

Throughout *all* this healing process I've been through, I've learned many, many important life and spiritual lessons. One thing that I learned is that you can be held in place simply by the reminder of every single thing that strikes out at you. As I was pondering these issues, a message again came to me in the form of a song which I had not heard of, or thought of in years. The song is called *The Boxer*, a famous song by Simon and Garfunkle. They chose not to change a word on the few lines of the song that came to me, but simply helped me in my understanding of it.

The lines of the song that came to me were as follows:

"In a clearing stands a boxer, and a fighter by his trade

And he carries the reminder of every glove that laid him down or cut him

'Til he cried out in his anger and his shame

'I am leaving, I am leaving,' but the fighter still remains"

It will take lots of emotional, mental, spiritual and, frankly, physical work, too, to let go of the reminder of every glove that laid you down and cut you until you cried out in your anger and your shame, dear reader. It becomes very easy, when you're dealing with trauma to continue carrying the reminder of every glove, or every issue, every moment that laid you down and cut you, until you cried out in your anger, shame, pain, disappointment, difficult feelings. I am not suggesting for a moment that you bottle up your emotions. Of course not. That's a really an important part of the process of moving forward.

Have your feelings. They're a part of you. But really, really work to let go of carrying these reminders with you, as a part of who you are. Learn from them. Learn the life, or spiritual lessons that they hold for you, and then let them go. Again, dear reader, this may take a therapist's help, or it may take the help of a loved one to keep you from carrying these reminders. But do try not to let them weigh heavily on your heart. They are a part of one of the valleys of your life. You need not dwell in one of the niches or caves within that valley. Leave it, to find what still remains and you can make whatever remains better and better. But, as I said, please do not dwell in the cave that simply is a reminder of every glove that laid you down. Kccp going. Ponder every reminder, sift through it, talk it out, learn the lessons it held for you, and keep on keepin'on.

Chapter Twenty-Three
You Can't Take That
Away From Me

The next message came to me as I was thinking of my dear, sweet Mama, who had made her transition in 1997. I was thinking of her, missing her and sending her love and thanks for the healing and messages that she was sending down to me, along with my other Master Teachers and guardian angels. Suddenly I heard a song in my head. It was a song of my Mama's generation, so no doubt it was her. The message I received was as follows:

"The way you wear your hat,
   the way you sing off key
The memory of all that —
   No, no they can't take that away from me"

Basically, it was Mama's way of telling me that she hadn't forgotten me, that she was thinking of me constantly and sending me all the healing and help she could from above.

The fact is, dear reader, when I was going through chemotherapy, I, as most people do, lost all my hair. So I did wear a hat to keep my poor, little, tiny bald head from freezing. And, frankly, even though I do sing, I actually often sing off key, unfortunately! Again, to me it was just Mama's way of saying that she held me in her heart. And, of course, she had memories of me, but also she was very much present with me as I was going through this terrible health trauma.

You have loved ones, too, dear reader, whom are going through this terrible trauma with you. They could be loved ones on this Earth plane, or loved ones on the heavenly planes of life. Regardless of where they are, they are there for you. They know you, they remember you, they think of you constantly, and they're sending their healing help. They are reaching out to hold your hand, and move you forward on the path of life. The memory of you can never be taken away from them. And, dear reader, even if you sing off key, too, don't worry about it, it's okay!

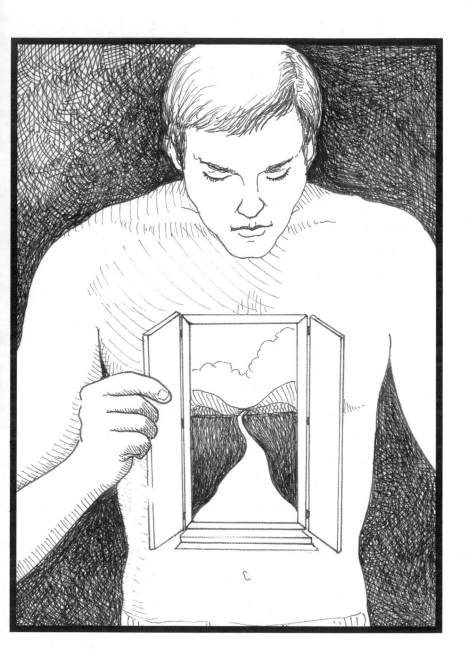

Chapter Twenty-Four
No, You Don't Know Me

The next message I received came to me as I was walking out of a physical therapy appointment. These messages of encouragement often come to me right after I have done something to help myself, or to strengthen my body.

The message I received at that point in time was:

Again, several lines from a famous song —

"You give your hand to me,
    and then you say 'goodbye'
I watch you walk away
Beside the lucky guy
You'll never, ever know
The one who loves you so
No, you don't know me"

And this of course in many ways is true. We don't really know ourselves fully and intensely until we turn our focus and our energy inward and ask for help. So again, no matter which one of life's traumas you may be going through, perhaps think of it as a tool to really get to know yourself, and to try to gain inner insight and growth while you're going through whatever of life's traumas this may be. It is a time to turn inward. Not only inward, of course, but more deeply perhaps than you have in the past.

It may have happened that you were so busy attempting to help others, which of course is important, that you have forgotten to pay attention to your own inner spiritual, emotional, mental and physical needs, as well. No matter what good we are attempting to achieve in this life for others it is important to add ourselves, and our own needs to the mix. Since I was a marriage and family therapist, I was so busy trying to work and help others, either get their relationships into a better place, or themselves to a better place that I forgot to really pay attention to my own needs. Don't forget, dear reader, even if you're not dealing with difficult traumas. Think of your own needs, as well as those of others. Give yourself some private time or some time with people that love you, doing things that make you happy.

My suggestion is, don't simply leave your focus to the outside, but turn inside, often and regularly. Use this particular life trauma that you may be dealing with to turn inward, to gain insight and growth on your own path. Know yourself, dear reader. Give yourself your own hand, and walk yourself upward along the physical, mental, emotional and spiritual paths. Know yourself, dear reader, and help yourself, as well as asking for help from others around you, and those above you.

Chapter Twenty-Five
Against All Odds
(Take a Look at Me Now)

The next message came to me when I was looking at myself in the mirror. There was my new self. I had lost a lot of weight due to chemotherapy and radiation. Though I had been bald, my hair had grown out again. But even though I had hair, it did not look like what it used to. A part of me felt, while looking at myself in the mirror, "Gee, it's wonderful that I'm still here, but who is this person? It's someone much thinner, with different hair, and a different look than I am used to seeing."

The lines that came to me were from the song, *Against All Odds*, and the message I received is as follows:

"Take a look at me now,
There's just an empty space
Nothing left there to remind me
Just a memory of your face
So take a look at me now
There's just an empty space
You're coming back to me is against all odds
But it's what I'll have to face"

This, of course, was written as a romantic song, but I believe the reason that they sent it to me was in regards to my self esteem. For example, I think about the way I looked in pictures before this happened to me. Clearly I had my strength, and my equilibrium. I'm not saying I was a super model, dear reader, nothing of the sort. But I was myself. My ability to get back to something close to that is against all odds. And for you, your ability to get back to something like your normal life before the ups and downs really hit you hard, may be against all odds. But, <u>you</u> are a little engine that can. Remember as a child perhaps you heard about the little engine that could. The train engine went up hill thinking, "I think I can, I think I can, I think I can." And it charges its way on up the hill. My suggestion to you, dear reader, is to change that to, a daily affirmation such as "I know I can, I know I can, I know I can."

Believe it or not, you can come back to yourself, even better than you once were. I'm not at all saying that I look better, but at least I'm here, and I do feel like I am better in some ways. Not my outer looks, but my inner spiritual understanding of all the trauma that life can bring.

Can good come back to you, dear reader, even against all odds? You bet it can. You're a little engine that can, no matter what. It may be against all odds, but with your own help, the help of those around you and those above you, you can keep charging yourself up that mountain.

Chapter Twenty-Six
Knockin' On Heaven's Door

The next message that came to me was from a song of my generation. Although, it did refer to my Mama, or to anyone's mother. It was a line from the song, *Knocking On Heaven's Door*, by Bob Dylan. The one line from the song that I received was:

"Mama take this badge from me
I can't use it anymore"

Basically, the line from this song was in regard to my prayers to Mama, other guardian angels and Master Teachers to release me from this brain tumor. I asked help to release shame, guilt and sadness. I don't need them anymore. Yes, of course for mc it was important to feel all those emotions as I was going through them. But it was also important for me not to get stuck there. I needed Mama's help, and the help of others to take this badge (metaphor for these intense feelings) off of me. I didn't need it anymore.

In a way, I may well have been knock, knock, knocking on heaven's door. I may have been closer than I know to passing, or tansitioning up to heaven. But regardless of whether that's true or not, I wore the badge of shame, guilt and sadness for quite a long time. This emotional badge, I mean. I do not need it anymore because I felt *all* those emotions, I went through them, I was able to let them go and move forward with a new badge and a new body, consisting of new emotional, physical, mental and spiritual health.

So, dear reader, it is my suggestion that whatever trauma you may dealing with, ask for help. Help in not only feeling in depth whatever feelings you may be confronted with. Ask for help in going through them, feeling them and removing them from your life. Do not continue to simply stay there in one place focusing on them. Feel them intensely, think them through, perhaps write them out fully and then burn them, talk them out and get help to let them go. Take that badge off of you, dear reader, you don't need it anymore. You're going forward.

Chapter Twenty-Seven
Fever

Although the previous message was not from Mama's generation, the next message that I received was. And, again, all these messages were voices in my head that I could hear singing. They mainly chose song as a way to communicate deeply with me, so I understood what they were trying to tell me. The message this time was as follows. Of course there were several words changed in each line to show the depth of their intent. The message was:

"You'll never know how much they love you
You'll never know how much they care
And when they put their arms around you
They send you healing that's not hard to bare
They send you healing when they kiss you
Healing when they hold you tight
Healing in the morning
Healing all through the night
They send you healing"

This, of course you may recognize is based on the famous song by Peggy Lee titled, *Fever*. Do know, dear reader, that your loved ones, your guardian angels and Master Teachers are there to love you, care for you, put their wings around you, and send you healing. Whether we feel it or not, whether we're aware of it or not, they're sending healing both in the morning, all through the day, and all through the night.

My suggestion is that you do your best to open up to receive this healing, through opening up your chakras during meditation, prayer, yoga, or something of this sort. Be open to the receiving of the wonderful, divine healing that they're sending to you. Oftentimes we are so busy focused on other things that we tend to block the healing process. That Divine, Sacred Light Energy is often not fully being received by our bodies, emotions, or hearts. My suggestion is that you take the time and enter into a healing process which helps you open up your body, heart, mind and soul to the wonderful healing energy that they are sending you.

Chapter Twenty-Eight
Free At Last

The last message that I received came to me after I had finally made some really, really good, important progress through physical therapy, wonderful Western medical doctors, and through the help of such alternative medical healing as Reiki, total body modification, bio-technical craniosacral, chiropractic, biofeedback, accupuncture, and my own process of prayer and meditation.

The message that came to me was one of the famous lines from Dr. Martin Luther King's wonderful "I Have a Dream" speech. The message was:

"Free at last, free at last, thank God Almighty, I am free at last."

And I do thank God Almighty, dear reader, that I am free at last. Free at last, from this *dreadful* brain tumor, and from the dreadful process of chemotherapy and radiation that I had to endure to free myself. But, of course, dear reader, I did not free myself alone. I worked every nano second that I could to help get free of this. And I asked for divine help, and for the help of a wonderful, loving support group that I had around me. Thank God that this support group is still with me both on this Earth plane, and above, in heaven. And thank God, I am free at last.

I did learn important spiritual lessons, and life lessons going through this process. And I'm sure you will learn these sort of lessons going through your own process. But, dear reader, whatever you may be going through, just know you will reach a point in your process where you, too, are free at last, free at last. Thank God Almighty, you are free at last.

Thank you, dear reader, for listening to these wonderful messages that my guardian angels, Master Teachers and my dear, sweet Mama sent to me over time.

My wish is that they be of important help to you, no matter what difficulty you may be facing.

Just know, dear reader, with the help of loved ones around and above you, you, too, will be free at last to move forward, even better than before.

So be it.

Blessed be.

- - - - - - - - - - - -

Acknowledgments

"Hello Dolly" (from the musical production), music and lyrics by Jerry Herman. ©1991 Jerry Herman.

"Big Spender" (from the musical comedy "Sweet Charity), music by Cy Coleman, lyrics by Dorothy Fields. ©1966 Dorothy Fields (lyrics).

"Darktown Strutter's Ball" words and music by Shelton Brooks (1917).

"Angel Of The Morning" words and music by Chip Taylor. ©1995 Chip Taylor.

"You Are My Sunshine" words by Otis D. Morris & Milton W. Kaiser, music by Jimmie Davis & Charles Mitchell. ©1981 Otis D. Morris.

"Rainy Day People" words and music by Dion DiMucci. ©2000 Dion DiMucci.

"The Rose" words and music by Amanda McBroom. ©1980 Fox Fanfare Music, Inc.

"Dancing In The Dark" words and music by Bruce Springsteen. ©1984 Bruce Springsteen.

"I Have Confidence" words and music by Richard Rodgers. ©1992 Dorothy Rodgers (words).

"It's Been A Long, Long Time" by Sammy Cahn and Jule Styne (1945).

A MESSAGE FROM
ASTARA

The publishers of this book have made it available to you in the belief that it will make a contribution to your life on its various important levels: physical, emotional, intellectual, and spiritual.

Astara was founded in 1951 as a non-profit religious and educational organization including the following concepts:

1. A center of all religions oriented to mystical teachings of ancient wisdom of every religion.

2. A school of the ancient Mysteries offering a compendium of the esoteric teachings of all ages.

3. A school of all philosophies coordinating many viewpoints of humankind and the interacting inner structures which unite us as one in the Infinite.

4. An center of metaphysical research and practice dedicated to physical, emotional and spiritual healing and wholeness.

If these areas of interest are appealing to you, you may wish to pursue the studies of *Astara's Book of Life* as have thousands of others in some ninety countries around the world.

To give you information about Astara, its teachings, and other possible services to you, we have prepared a treatise entitled *If You Are a Seeker*. You may have it without cost or obligation. Write:

Astara
10700 Jersey Blvd., Ste. 450
P.O. Box 2100
Rancho Cucamonga, CA 91729-2100
Phone: (909) 948-7412
Fax: (909) 948-2016
E-Mail: mail@astara.org
Website: www.astara.org